To my beautiful Mum,

Love you Loads,

Hope you enjoy this book.

Love your one and

only daughter.

I dedicate this book to the most important person in the world, YOU.

GW00674622

Raja is the founder of the PAN Academy and the originator of the HELP (Human Evolution and Life Procreation) Programme.

Born and raised in Africa, he spent his childhood playing in the wilderness, observing the drama of nature. Raja's mother encouraged him, in these crucial years, to absorb and value these experiences. She died when he was fourteen and it was at this time he decided to embark on a voyage of discovery. From then on he travelled and worked in Europe, Africa and Asia. In these years he was often penniless and frequently sleeping outdoors. With him he carried a small book of inspirations which he had collected on the way. In moments of doubt and desperation he would contemplate on an inspiration and lift himself out of inertia.

The purpose of writing this book is to empower young people and to conduct 'Living Inspirations' seminars for schools and youth organizations.

At present, Raja lives in Cornwall and teaches at the Pan Academy.

LIVING INSPIRATIONS

A Classic Companion for Life

RAJA

ELEMENT

Shaftesbury, Dorset ● Rockport, Massachusetts
Brisbane, Queensland

© Planetary Alliance Network, Inc. 1994

First published in Great Britain in 1994 by
Element Books Ltd
Shaftesbury, Dorset

Published in the USA in 1994 by
Element, Inc.
42 Broadway, Rockport, MA 01966

Published in Australia in 1994 by
Element Books Ltd
for Jacaranda Wiley Ltd
33 Park Road, Milton, Brisbane, 4064

Cover design by Bridgewater Books
Edited by Jane O'Neil
Typeset by Matthew Davison
Printed and bound in Great Britain by
Hartnolls Limited, Bodmin, Cornwall

British Library Cataloguing in Publication
data available

Library of Congress Cataloging in Publication
data available

Created by Raja

ISBN 1-85230-557-6

CONTENTS

In Appreciation

Living Inspirations was made possible by the collective wisdom of humanity. I am grateful to all those whose words are included in this anthology and to numerous people whose efforts have influenced my views and my selections, even though their names have not been included.

I am grateful also to the publishers who have permitted the publication of this book.

I dedicate this book to the most important person in the world . . . YOU.

Raja

PREFACE

Inspiration is seeing with every part of ourselves. From our physical eyes to our feelings, thoughts, dreams, creative insight and spiritual unfolding. Inspiration permeates all our life experiences. And it is ours to keep!

If we regard inspiration in this broadened holistic way, it gives us the doorway and the knowledge to evolve and improve our daily lives:

> Why must life only roll downhill
> and then be irretrievable?

There must be a better way! Fortunately for those of us who want to awaken and be progressive throughout our life, to be full of excitement and beauty, replete with 'aha' and 'I see that clearly now', there are answers. We are able to keep, improve, develop and expand our life's visions and actions through our own inspiration.

Inspiration is important to all of us. When life becomes dull, unbalanced, blurred, unhealthy, we want to be able to do something about it. This book provides an avenue for you to travel on – a journey in which you can learn about and renew your total outlook on life.

Many benefits are to be derived from nurturing your inspirational process. These have to do with release of anxiety, depression and so on. One inspiration can change our perspective of the pain and suffering that often stems from fear, sorrow of separation, disease and suicidal tendencies. Inspiration gives us hope and rebuilds our will power, to break free from inertia.

No matter how powerful we are, sooner or later we all need to be inspired to go forward. So, this book is for everyone. Its ideas are to be used everywhere. The whole world has provided these pearls of wisdom.

How to use this Book

In the fast-moving world we live in, we do not take the time to relax and reflect. Consequently we lose the purpose and direction of our lives and end up going nowhere very fast.

The following steps will enable you to transform the words in this book into priceless pearls of wisdom.

1. Read slowly

By reading this book slowly, you will multiply its value. One word or inspiration is often enough.

Read one point or inspiration a day or a week.

2. Contemplate quietly

Contemplation is seeing with your mind's eye. It gives you an overview and helps you to get our world into perspective.

Mornings or before bed are the best moments to contemplate.

3. Feel wholeheartedly

When thoughts are emotionalized, they become magnetized and fill you up with beauty and power. You feel inspired and a deep sense of compassion soothes your heart.

Place one or both of your palms on your chest.

4. Breathe deeply

Inspiration needs respiration – so take deep breaths. Consciousness is like a kite and breath simply guides it.

Close your eyes and breathe into your belly, mid chest and upper chest – then exhale freely.

5. Use the book lovingly

How you use this book will show you how you use yourself and others. Receive each word for yourself, without the thought of hoarding, re-using or sharing. As you become full, you will overflow and everything will happen as though by 'magic'.

Once you feel the truth, beauty and power of the 'word', it becomes active and alive. And it stays active for the rest of your life.

LIFE

We are all philosophers of life and we are all concerned to some degree about the origin, nature and destiny of life. At best, such interest and inquiry can only satisfy academic questions. What people are really eager to know is how to extract the most contentment, satisfaction and fulfilment from their own lives. The hard-pressed individual of today, surrounded with the most elaborate set of practical problems, is anxious to live life to the full. You and I are aware that the gift of life is miraculous and want to make the most of our allotted time. We pass quickly through restless, hurried, anxious days and call it 'living', thinking if we capture a passing thrill now and then that is 'Life'. Deep in our hearts, however, we know that real life is better than that. It is a great and wonderful experience which *can* be created.

Many of us miss the joy of life; we can become taken up by our everyday routines and cares and so are merely alive instead of living. Too busy. Hamlet is not the only man to have found his days 'stale, fraught and unprofitable'. Is time running out for you? Do you feel that in some way you are missing out on life's pleasures? This sense of unfulfilment and regret does not have to be the case. It is possible to lead a full life with peace of mind and to let our personalities loose on the world.

Life has a habit of hitting us at point-blank range – like a kid with a water pistol. Most of the time we are dodging the water pistol, swerving and weaving and taking the shocks and blows, tending to be reactive to events rather than initiating our own real intentions and enjoying life. We spend too much time anticipating the blows, such as retirement or death of a relative. We also spend too much time preparing and planning for these and other events – holidays for example. So much time is spent on planning and preparation and yet the event itself is often empty and unsatisfying.

We need to relearn how to enjoy the moments.

We need to learn to live in the present moment; to be conscious of what is happening *now*: the sun shining on our faces, meeting a friend and sharing lovely food. We need to enjoy the quiet, simple moments. Life's pleasures are so basic – forget the striving after the illusions of wealth and status, the rich are just as prone to being alive and not living as the poor. Life is an art, and to be successful you have to know the real from the imitation and be content with the fineness of quality. Peace of mind is worth any amount of riches. Each day should be treated as a new day, for every morning we are reborn. Leave behind yesterday's catalogue of frustrations, petty resentments and jealousies. Let them drop like leaves off a tree.

There are other reasons why we cannot live life fully. We may not believe in ourselves. This results in weak, ineffectual and even impotent human beings instead of strong, dynamic and creative ones. The solution for many in this case is to develop a wholesome self-appreciation. To cultivate a genuine understanding of the worth and significance of yourself and all people. In today's high-tech society emphasis is placed on machines, profits and growth – we have relegated ourselves to be their slaves when they should be ours. In each of us, there is a wonder and beauty comparable to the majesty and magnificence of the universe.

Worry and anxiety is another life negator. At worst it can lead to physical ill-health. Our spirits can grow gray before our hair. One of the best ways to relieve worry and the storing-up of troubles is simply to exercise your body. It's so simple! Working up a sweat is therapeutic and also calms the mind and emotions so that your problems can be put into perspective. Every problem carries its own solution, by not facing and dealing with them we fill our lives with anxiety.

We also have to take time to live: get off the hamster's wheel we are on and do things we want to do, not what others want us to. The phone rings and we often find ourselves jumping to the wishes of other people. Be true to yourself; have the honesty and take the freedom to say no. Learn to do 'nothing' – spend time with yourself.

In these ways we will come to know ourselves better. Life begins for the person who meets himself. To feel you are living is to know yourself and to experience your own being – reveal yourself to yourself. Don't submerge your personality beneath a blanket of routine and undesired actions and goals which society dictates. Have the courage to be yourself and live!

Look to this day for it is life.
The very life of life.
In its brief course
lie all the realities and truths of existence.
The joy of growth,
the splendour of action,
the glory of power.
For yesterday is but a memory
and tomorrow is only a vision.
But today well lived
makes every yesterday a memory of joy
and every tomorrow a vision of hope.
Look well, therefore, to this day.

Do more than exist, live.
Do more than touch, feel.
Do more than look, observe.
Do more than read, absorb.
Do more than hear, listen.
Do more than listen, understand.

*Life is a daring adventure,
or nothing at all.*

*No objects of value
are worth the priceless experience
of waking up one more day.*

We cannot put off living until we are ready.
The most salient characteristic of life
is its coerciveness;
it is always urgent, 'here and now',
without any possible postponement.
Life is fired at us point blank.

*Always remember that the future
comes one day at a time.*

*To achieve great things we must live as though
we were never going to die.*

We do not understand that life is paradise,
for it suffices only to wish to understand it,
and at once paradise will appear in front of us
in its beauty.

How soon will you realize that the only thing
you don't have,
is the direct experience that there is nothing you need
that you don't have?

I shall pass this way but once;
any good therefore, that I can do
or any kindness that I can show,
to any human being, let me do it now.
Let me not defer nor neglect it
for I shall not pass this way again.

The power of life and death lies in the tongue.

Be still; for life cannot be fetched.

The clouds above us join and separate,
the leaves in the courtyard leave and return.
Life is like that, so why not relax.
Who can stop us from celebrating?

I take no action
and people are reformed.
I enjoy peace
and people become honest.
I use no force
and people grow rich.
I have no ambitions
and people return to the good and simple life.

There is no wealth but life.

All things come to he who waits.

*The greatest gift you can give to others
is the example of your own life working.*

LOVE

ALL you need is love, love is all you need.'
'Love is the answer.' No aspect of human
existence has been celebrated more in song,
literature or the arts than love.

Radio, TV, and the other media constantly
bombard us with images about love. It seems our
society is obsessed with this thing called love – in all
its manifestations, erotic, spiritual, intimate,
passionate and parental, to name but a few. Society
reflects our own preoccupation with love; it is
undoubtedly the ultimate and real need in every
human being. Mankind's desire for interpersonal
fusion is its most powerful striving and the fulfilment
of this desire in each of us *is* the answer to human
existence, not just with our partner but on a wider
range, with friends and people we meet. Imagine
what a society we would have if we really loved each
other! Would we still need to say 'I love you'?

Despite this need within us all, love is an area of
our lives that remains unfulfilled. The list of love

problems are numerous – they come under the categories of misuse, abuse, over-use and non-use. The problem lies in the attitude we have towards love; we all seek to have love or to be loved when, in fact, it is a quality or an ability. What we need to strive for is the capacity to love others – it's not a commodity, it's a capacity! Viewed from this perspective the aim is to love others, not to gain love.

We live in a world where everything is dominated by economics and the market place, where the means have replaced the ultimate goals, so that people strive for money which they believe will give them fulfilment, comfort and ease. So it is with love; we have become preoccupied with acquiring the trappings which we feel will bring us affection. Men generally strive for wealth, power and status; women tend to be more concerned with their physical appearance, safety and stability. Both sexes look at themselves as commodities, and each attribute to themselves and others, unconsciously, a market value – what they are worth. They then seek an object whom they feel has a high enough value to be worthy of their love.

By looking at love as a capacity, it is clear that it is something we can all strive to learn, not merely a pleasant sensation that we 'fall into' if we're lucky.

Surely this 'pleasant sensation' is only a small part of love; yet many take it to be love itself. By concentrating on our capacity to love others we immediately begin to recognize the capacity of others to give love; so in the act of loving we become experts in receiving it as well. In this way what we crave comes to us in the process of learning to love others. The more we love, the more love we can recognize and receive! By learning to love unconditionally we can also receive love unconditionally, that is without any feelings of obligation, of having to do something in return.

The first step must be to love ourselves. Self-love is not an arrogant conceit but a genuine and honest understanding of ourselves and our needs. We need to recognize our needs in the three areas of which we are all composed, the body, mind and emotions. Too often we do not respond to our needs – we make do with situations in which we are not happy or fulfilled and fob ourselves off with excuses as to why this situation exists when it is our own responsibility. By listening to our needs and acting on them improvements can be made. Courage is required. There is everything to gain and only the present dissatisfaction to lose.

By being aware of our bodily requirements in terms of touch, sensation and stimulation and how we use our bodies in action, we can exercise control and conserve our energy. This increase in energy and self-awareness makes us more sensitive to the needs of others. We have to communicate to our partners what we want. At its best, sexual union can lead to a feeling of being reborn and of fusing completely with your partner and of 'losing' your own identity. We also need to pay attention to our hearts – what do we want in intimacy, passion and compassion? As regards our spiritual side, that too must be satisfied – what is more spiritual than creating and raising another human being?

In the world in which we live, opportunities to love are increasingly difficult to find. Society is organized in such a way that for the majority there is less and less social contact. In our isolation, we seek consolation in the acquisition of material 'benefits' – a poor temporal substitute for interpersonal union and a sense of community. Remember, the stranger next to you in the city has the same wishes as you – so make an effort to meet people.

Remember, the person who gives love freely is richer than the person who hoards love.

Who loves you?
And who do you love?

There is no enterprise which starts
with such tremendous hopes and expectations
and which fails so regularly as romantic love.

A union of man and woman is like the mating
of Heaven and Earth. It is because of their correct
mating that Heaven and Earth last for ever.
Humans have lost this secret and have therefore
become mortal.
By knowing it, the Path to Immortality is opened.

Big man
small man
help the little man.

I will show the strength with my word.
I will show the way of the heart.
I will serve the proud in their
imagination of the heart.
I will free the mighty from their seats.
I will exalt the lowly.
I will fill the hungry with good things,
And send no one away empty.
I am going to set at liberty those who are oppressed
And proclaim the age of paradise.

All things grow with time except grief.

*Happiness in marriage
is entirely a matter of chance.*

Though I speak with the tongues of men and angels,
but have not love,
I am a noisy gong or a clanging cymbal.
And if I have prophetic powers
and understand all mysteries and all knowledge...
but not have love, I am nothing.
And if I have all faith,
and so to remove mountains,
but have not love, I am nothing.
If I deliver my body to be burned,
but have not love, I gain nothing.

*The hunt isn't over until both your heart
and your belly are full.*

*A loving person lives in a loving world,
a hostile person lives in a hostile world.
Everyone you meet is your mirror.*

Deep at the centre of my being there is an infinite well of love. I now allow this love to flow to the surface —it fills my heart, my body, my mind, my consciousness, my very being, and radiates out from me in all directions and returns to me multiplied. The more love I use and give, the more I have to give, the supply is endless.

The use of love makes me feel good, it is an expression of my inner joy. I love myself, therefore I take loving care of my body.

I lovingly feed it nourishing foods and beverages. I lovingly groom it and dress it, and my body lovingly responds to me with vibrant health and energy.

I love myself, therefore I provide for myself a comfortable home, one that fills all my needs and is a pleasure to be in. I fill the rooms with the vibration of love so that all who enter, myself included, will feel nourished by it.

I love myself therefore I work at a job that I truly enjoy doing, one that uses my creative talents and abilities, working with and for people that I love and that love me, earning a good income.
I love myself therefore I behave and think in a loving way to all people for I know that that which I give out returns to me multiplied.
I only attract loving people in my world for they are a mirror of what I am.
I love myself therefore I forgive myself totally and release the past and all past experiences and I am free.
I love myself, therefore I love totally in the now, experiencing each moment as good and knowing that my future is bright, joyous, and secure, for I am a beloved child of the universe and the universe lovingly takes care of me now and forever more.
And so it is.

I love mankind
It's people I can't stand.

A woman can draw you
further than dynamite can blow you.

Love is a trembling happiness.

Love of others and love of ourselves are not
alternatives.
On the contary, an attitude of love
towards themselves will be found
in all those who are capable of loving others.

NATURE

Nature is that which we have sprung from and to which we owe our existence. We are a part of nature – how we treat nature is how we treat ourselves. Nature has therefore been of fundamental importance to mankind throughout history. It has been an inspiration, an interest and, more recently, a concern. Our reliance on nature is total! It provides us with what we require to live and breathe; no wonder it has been worshipped and deified in the past. It has evolved gradually since the dawn of time some 4.5 billion years ago. On the scale of a biological twenty-four hour clock it is now 2400 hours and mankind has turned up in the last three minutes. It is a terrible indictment of us all that, in that short time, we have dominated and used nature as an inexhaustible resource for our selfish, limited purposes. We cannot go on exploiting the Earth's resources at the present rate; if we do, nature will take steps to return to a natural harmony, which may not have mankind as part of it. This view of nature sees nature as a unified and harmonic entity, a self-sustaining whole composed of subordinate wholes, each having a life and nature of its own, but so adjusted that while it pursues its private end it also functions in the interest of the systems that contain it. It is known as the 'Gaia theory', named after an old pagan goddess and sees the Earth as a living organism, a system in which each part is ordered with a view to the perfection of the whole. Time is of the essence. Hopefully mankind's resourcefulness and action in the face of threat will preserve us. It starts with you.

Our society is organized so that millions of us living in cities have become separated from nature and have little experience and appreciation of it. We just don't have enough contact with fresh air, the soil, fire and water. We are largely leading unnatural lives in the city, divorced from the elements that we spring from and of which we consist. To a lot of people the concept of hugging a tree is so alien that it seems laughable. Children do it naturally. The tropical rainforests would not be so endangered if there was a real and genuine concern for trees through experiencing them from an early age. The need to dominate nature springs from a fear of nature – it seems that nature cannot be tolerated in the cities. There are a few green spaces, gardens and parks, but how many of us are comfortable with an absence of street lighting? How many of us see the outdoors as full of threats such as winds, coldness, rain and 'wild' animals and strange noises?

Most of us are not so divorced from nature that we can't appreciate it – when it's safe and looks like the picture on a chocolate box, and also when the car is nearby. In fact there is a real craving within each of us to have that closer communion with nature which our forefathers had. The vision of paradise in so many civilizations has been the garden – lush with abundant vegetation, with clear, fresh flowing rivers and a picturesque landscape brightened with birdsong. We instinctively feel that such a place is beautiful and 'right' – it is our inner voice that responds to our surroundings and says that this isharmony. To stop treating nature as a dustbin and an inexhaustible resource we have to get in touch once again with this voice. The nice thing is that in making the effort to develop an affinity we benefit in so many ways. The effect of a simple walk in the countryside has tremendous therapeutic consequences for a person's well-being; it refreshes and invigorates the body, calms and soothes the mind and balances the emotions. Let us bring nature back into our lives.

There is such wealth in nature that can contribute

to our lives. Scientists, artists and scholars have all studied and been fascinated and inspired by nature. Art has always attempted to capture or mimic nature – if we can take time to visit galleries we should be open to the wonderful scenes that surround us. Nature has also provided us with medicines and vaccines, the more it has been studied the more miraculous it appears. We all have a deep-rooted desire to know our origin – it has been said that every man must know the foundation he is treading on so that his stride becomes secure and bold; by getting in touch with nature we therefore become more secure. As a result our respect for nature will grow.

The earth gave birth to us. It continues to nurture and provide for us, we are free to use and abuse it. The way we treat our planet is the way we treat ourselves.

One impulse from the vernal wood may teach you
more of man, of moral evil and of good,
than all the sages can.

When nature has work to be done
she creates a genius to do it.

*Never does nature say one thing
and wisdom another.*

*The more materials you have
the less freedom you have.*

Entering the forest without
moving the grass;
Entering the water without
raising a ripple.

Much silence makes a mighty noise.

Where there is honey
there are fierce stinging bees.

If you lie down with dogs
you get up with fleas.

Don't push the river.
Let it flow.

Every thousand moons a truth teller is born.
That person tells the truth regardless
of the consequences.

A day in the country
is worth a month in the town.

The art of medicine consists of amusing
the patient whilst nature cures the disease.

Nature admits no lie.

All moons,
all years,
all days,
all winds
take their course and pass away.

*Everything that isn't indispensable
is useless.*

*The only thing we have to fear on the planet
is man.*

CHARACTER

One aspect of our lives that we seem to take for granted is that of the rich diverseness of humanity. In an age when there is pressure to conform to accepted behaviour, let's have the courage to be who we are and let our character shine through. The aim is to get in contact with our real selves, perhaps buried away beneath behaviour induced and expected in us by our parents and society. When the chips are down, in moments of crisis, our true selves often rise to the surface. Let's allow this character to be present with us throughout our lives.

The great panoply of human characteristics that are found in each of us is what unites us in a common bond with our neighbours, from the gentle traits of compassion and caring to aggression, persistence and ruthlessness. Each are of value and not better or worse than the other. Let us appreciate our own unique character, and become aware of the ever changing kaleidoscope of characteristics that makes us what we are. If we recognize our strengths and weaknesses honestly, and accept them with no feelings of regret or of arrogance, we begin to really know ourselves. We should accept ourselves for what we are and give our characteristics full play; why hide our light under a bushel? Let us also have the courage to acknowledge our faults; how, otherwise, can we improve and grow?

With this self-knowledge we are capable of appreciating and taking an interest in other people. We can delight and admire the character of other people long since departed and be able to relate to them on a personal level. Strangely, it is often the human weaknesses of others that we delight in, perhaps gaining reassurance that we are not alone in having faults. When we become more conscious of humanity and all its facets, this will arm us with clarity and insight when evaluating others. Such knowledge will have an immense bearing on us in terms of who we call our friends, and in our choice of partner. Appropriate decisions will be made.

We are, of course, to some degree products of our environment and upbringing. Yet we all have the capacity of free will. Determination and courage will enable us, if we will it, to break free of the shackles which prevent us from being our true selves. Change of character is more the norm than the exception. It is a constant process of asking yourself, 'Why am I behaving like this?' and 'Do I want this?' 'If not, what is it I want?' By asking these questions we come to a better understanding of ourselves.

The door then becomes open for self-improvement or 'growth'. We can pinpoint any weakness in our character, such as sloth, insincerity and lack of commitment, and go out and consciously improve ourselves. This ability to recognize ourselves and say 'This is me' and to be content with that, is the road to self-love and the love of others. With self-knowledge we soon become aware of what we really want and need. Our lives are then richer and more fulfilled as we refocus our energies and direction to goals that are satisfying to us.

A strong character then, does not mean someone who can throw his weight around and bully other people. A strong character is not someone who dominates others and orders servants around. A strong character is an individual with a good idea of who and what he or she is. They can then act on this knowledge, knowing what they can or can't achieve, what is a challenge and what isn't. They have a clear idea as to what is their will. With the gift of 'will' and of self-knowledge about their personal limitations they are indeed strong characters. Once we know our limitations we can conquer them, get help from others, or slowly push back the boundaries ourselves – all geared to getting what I want from life with what I have at my disposal. Me!

A liar cannot trust anyone.

*It's not what you were,
it's what you are today.*

What you believe is what you are.
What you think is what you create.
What you say will happen to you.
What you love is what you receive.

Character is what you are in the dark.

Please all and you will please no one.

The larva that crawls through the dung
later becomes a fire-fly
that lights the night.

Sayings remain meaningless
until they are embodied in habits.

I am not what you call me,
I am what I respond to.

The buck stops here.

The only difference between men and boys
is their toys.

However diverse their talents,
temperaments and differences,
all great achievers have one
trait in common:
they never bother to compare
themselves with other men,
but are content to run their
own race on their own terms.

When we lose the comfortable
formulas that have hitherto been our guides
amid the complexities of existence....
we feel like drowning in the ocean of confusion
until we find a new foothold or learn to swim.

A rich man is the man
who is satisfied with what he has.

People do not become great
by doing great things.
People do great things because they are great.

None but the coward dares to boast that
he has never known fear.

Our worst fault is our preoccupation
with the faults of others.

FRIENDSHIP

One of the most rewarding gifts anyone can have is friendship. As people grow older, however, friends disappear slowly and become fewer and fewer. Friends you can be close with, friends you can express yourself freely to and who can confide in you. People who will accept you as you are and in whom you can place your trust. Friends who can advise and comfort you in times of trouble, and friends who can turn around and point out your shortcomings in a sensitive way for your benefit. Yes, a true friend will tell you things you may not want to hear about yourself. Conversely, you should be able to give them advice, free of any fears of rejection.

We all want, at times, someone to turn to, someone to share our joys and sorrows, someone who likes us and whom we like and can open ourselves up to. The world today, with it's mobile populations chasing work and better lifestyles, seems to make the process of finding a friend more difficult. Loneliness has become a major social problem with thousands feeling isolated and suicidal.

In the large urban sprawls, families and friends may live some distance away and contact may be lost. Friends move away or we may find ourselves in a new area not knowing anyone. Ironically, it's in cities with so many people and so much activity that quality friendships are most lacking.

If you find yourself without a friend do something about it. No one is going to knock on your door and ask to be your friend, unless you are exceptionally lucky. We need to initiate action ourselves and overcome any fears of rejection or feelings of inadequacy. Chronic shyness can also be overcome in gradual steps. Don't be slow to get help – you only have one life and it would be a tragic waste to miss out on one of its greatest gifts. We need to cultivate self-esteem and a sense of our own worth. The lonely have largely themselves to blame for their predicament; it is all too easy to feel sorry for yourself and remain fixed and inactive.

There are so many routes open. Follow an interest you have and join an organization of like-minded individuals. You will automatically have something in common to start a conversation. Socialize more by accepting invitations to functions and take an interest in other people you talk to. They may want a friend too. Be sensitive to others – friendship is not only about taking but also about giving.

Friendships need to be worked at, like a garden they need regular attention and care. Neglect often leads to friendship degenerating into merely habitual acquaintance, where closeness is never really achieved, leading to unfulfilment on all sides. Another danger lies in being too intense, possessive and overbearing so that your partners are not allowed space to breathe and be themselves. Also take the freedom to end a relationship which you feel is inappropriate and you have now outgrown. People do change over the years, yet so many cling on to old friends perhaps through fear of not developing new ones. The person you knew at school may be totally different now.

In any new or existing relationship we should aim to bring the maximum of beauty to it. The more we reveal of ourselves the more we will increase intimacy on all sides. Realizing and preserving beauty in our relationships will greatly enrich our lives.

Maintaining a relationship is a skill. We all have demands on our time from wives and husbands and work. If we feel obliged to fulfil a marital or social engagement in preference to an activity with friends, we risk their disappointment. We are constantly juggling to satisfy all parties. You must remain sensitive to all involved; ultimately, how you spend your time will reveal your priorities.

As in all relationships, the key to success are the four Cs: commitment, compatibility, communication and companionship. Ideally, we should aim to give our partner and friends what we would like to receive. If we achieve harmony in these four areas our relationships will be rewarding, fulfilling and beautiful.

There are no strangers here,
only friends we have not met.

Wisdom will never let us stand with
any man or woman
on an unfriendly footing.

The most dangerous road of all
is called revenge.

If one does not wish for the truth,
the mirror becomes the enemy.

Do unto others
as you would be done by.

Hugging is a means of getting two people so close
that they can't see anything wrong with each other.

Love demands infinitely less
than friendship.

Always forgive your enemies –
nothing annoys them so much.

A constant friend is never welcome.

Do not judge
and you will not be judged.
Do not condemn,
and you will not be condemned.
Forgive,
and you will be forgiven.

No man can be friends
with a woman he finds attractive.

And Joseph had a dream
and he told it to his brethren,
and they hated him even more.

The hereafter brothers and sisters
is here and now.

It's no use trying to be clever —
we are all clever here;
just try to be kind — a little kind.

Never underestimate the capacity of a person
to say one thing and do another.

Where two or more are gathered,
that is home.

PLAY

Play? – It's for kids!' 'I haven't got time to play games!' We've all heard these things said at some point in our lives. It seems that play is trivial and unimportant and only secondary to serious things such as earning a living. People who use these phrases tend to be busy, intense, serious and disciplined individuals, just the sort of people you might expect to run efficient well-managed companies and organizations. It's strange then that some are incapable of managing their lives to incorporate one of the rich ingredients to human happiness and enjoyment.

The irony is that if we take more time to play, we seem to create more time for ourselves. Top executives have learnt this. Look at any group of decisionmakers in an organization – they are the people with the greatest leisure time, in quantity and quality. Company bosses can run their businesses from the golf course! So what does this appear to indicate about the role of play?

Surely the message must be that play and having a laugh and joke are vital if we want to work at optimum efficiency and be freely creative. The individual who does not consciously set aside time to play is often seen as a dour workaholic. Without playing we lose our sense of adventure and lack spontaneity. We're like horses running in a race with blinkers on – tunnel-visioned, incapable of appreciating what and who there is around us.

Play is distinct from leisure because it is spontaneous and unstructured. Organized sports such as football and tennis, through their conventional rules and an increasing 'win at all costs' mentality, are losing the element of play which leads to flair, skill and the introduction of the unusual. There is less room for personal expression – one of play's key elements.

Children have no problem playing – only in stopping! Their enjoyment is there for everyone to behold. By observing children at play we can learn so much about what it can do for us 'sophisticated adults'. Firstly there are the physical benefits, such as getting exercise and improving co-ordination and dexterity. For children it is also an exercise in learning about themselves and the world. They are constantly learning about the world outside themselves and in the process their minds are stimulated. They begin to put the world into perspective, for example in acting out scenarios and norms of behaviour. They also develop an interest in others, as reflected in dressing up as fire-fighters and nurses. Play is also vital for a child's personal growth. From thinking in terms of 'my toy' the child learns to share its toys and recognizes the limitation and reality of 'ownership'. They also learn to come to terms with the loss of a toy or a playmate. The act of playing helps us to grow up. The more we play the more we grow!

So how do we adults play? It can be in so many different ways. Try throwing acorns at a friend in the park and see what develops. The idea is not to escape into a video or a cinema but to break out of the fixed boundaries we learn from an early age. We need to let our imaginations have a free reign – to be child-like in having no fear of expression and to enjoy the simple joy of being. Play should be free of the fear of failure and loss. There are no yardsticks: only the freedom to break out of stereotyped behaviour – 'the same old things'. Play should help us hurdle the boundaries of preconceptions and overcome taboos. Play frees the adult to relive the experience of discovering himself and to create something unique and new. The play of lovers, in a safe and supportive partnership, allows the expression of emotions from rage and frustration to childishness and the need to be cherished, and can unlock the doors of self-discovery.

Life can be viewed as a game where the only yardstick of success is your own, not that of others. With such an attitude we become free from the rigid structures imposed on us and hence become more creative. For adults as well as children, play imparts a vitality and youthfulness which keeps us young at heart.

We can therefore learn from children as we apply ourselves to play. We can put that extra magic into our lives which enables us to be more creative – surely a prerequisite to a richer and fuller life. Play's de-stressing effect is like taking time out from the worries and pressures of everyday life; a time to recharge the batteries through the immersion of our imaginations and energies into another world of our own making. Let us play – Amen.

All sins come from playing to win.

It is almost as important to know
what is not serious
as to know what is.

It's not how many cards you have.
It's how you play them.

You can get as much fun out of a ball
as an expensive fast car.

Dear Pope,
If we are all children of God,
why don't the grown-ups play with me?

A fart is never funny when you're on your own.

The only game played without rules is politics.

Play is a man re-creating himself.

Half a leap falls in the ditch.

*The lack of play
leads to incompetence.*

*There is only one man
who does not make a mistake.
It's the man who doesn't do anything.*

One hour of playing
saves three hours of work.

All work and no play
makes Jack a dull boy!

I don't know what I may seem to the world.
But as to myself, I seem to have been only like
a boy playing on the seashore,
and diverting myself now and then finding a
smoother pebble or a prettier shell than ordinary,
whilst the great ocean of truth lay all
undiscovered before me.

Four and seventy years of a life of devotion.
Toil and tears have taught me how to pray.
The next time round I shall
play and not pray.

The surest way to remain a winner
is to win once
and then not play anymore!

VISION

All the great people in history have shared one thing – they possessed a strong vision of what they wanted. The strength of this belief has given people such as Gandhi, Martin Luther King and Emmeline Pankhurst, an incredible amount of energy to fulfil their visions. The vitality and devotion with which these individuals operate attracts like-minded people and support from others. Belief in a goal stands out like a beacon and will automatically attract others who share the vision. With a clear vision and 100 per cent commitment to it, mountains can and have been moved. It has been demonstrated that the poorest and simplest of us can accomplish wonders with such convictions. Once the vision is in place, along with determination and faith, no hurdle is too great to vault. A way is always found.

Everyone has been through the process of realizing a vision to some degree. Decorating a room is a similar process. You start with the vision, then find and do what you need to create it. On an individual level most of us can realize some visions. Where the greater visions are concerned, such as what sort of world we want to live in, things are not always so clear; if you don't have a clear vision, how can you make it real? We tend to stumble through life, busy with keeping mind and body together, surviving the shocks. A sense of visions and goals becomes submerged so that our lives have no sense of direction and purpose. Often the goal seems so large that we don't even bother trying – the fear of failure has deterred many. No matter how large the goal may seem, achieving it starts with small steps. Also remember that success lies in the journey, not in the destination. The fact that you are working to an end gives meaning and direction to your life. So don't be afraid of falling on your backside – with persistence you will find other routes to create your vision. You can always hold your head high and say, 'Well I tried'.

Too many of us are quite content to lead lives following a vision that has been fed to us. In today's consumer society it's in the interest of large companies to have a population striving for big houses, cars, TV sets, a villa in the sun and other carrots dangled in front of us. We chase these things like headless chickens. If this is the vision you are chasing then you had better take what goes along with it. A visit to any large city will show you what that is. Noise, overcrowding, polluted air and water. In this selfish chase, human beings are secondary to making money. A clean, comfortable place to urinate, the most basic of human functions, is way down on the list of priorities. *You* just aren't of primary consideration! So, if you do have a vision, make sure it serves you and everyone else.

You may also be guilty of accepting the status quo as being fixed and unalterable. We don't have to accept what exists as some sort of finality or truth. Think in terms of the possible! Both on individual and societal levels. How many people continue a relationship they are unhappy in because they think it is somehow set in concrete? How many of us accept that there are not enough homes for everyone to live in? It is us who create our own reality. As Schopenhauer said, 'The world is my idea.'

Is it only the special few in the past who have possessed the sustained moral dedication to question and change the world? No! You also can apply this sense of vision to your own life in varying degrees: individual, communal and societal. You can change so many little things: the way you look, the state of your home and, on a communal level, noise pollution, access for the disabled to buildings and so on.

You are that special person – the one in a million. All you may lack is a vision and direction. By contemplation and listening to our needs, vision is gained. This will automatically enrich your life, and help you become more creative in making the dream a reality. In the process of getting up and doing something, you will embark on a journey of discovery and knowledge. The human mind is the most powerful instrument known to us. You can employ it to serve you and your vision. The greatest buildings and the noblest of charities were all, at one time, an idea in someone's mind. Once the first step is taken the rest will follow. Have the courage to follow your dream and it will come true.

*An aim in life is the only fortune
worth finding.*

*No dream is too big to dream,
no truth is too good to be true.*

*Do not follow where the path may lead,
go instead where there is no path
and leave a trail.*

Drop by drop lakes are created.

To climb steep hills requires slow pace at first.

Success is the postponement of failure.

If you don't know where you are going,
you'll probably end up somewhere else.

To undertake a project,
as the word's derivation indicates,
means to cast an idea out ahead of oneself
so that it gains autonomy and is fulfilled
not only by the efforts of the originator,
indeed, independently of him as well.

The dream is the truth.

Whatever you can do, or dream you can
begin it.
Boldness has genius,
power and magic in it.

If you think you are beaten, you are
If you think you dare not, you don't
If you'd like to win, but think you can't
It's almost certain you won't.
If you think you'll lose, you've lost
For out of the world we find
Success begins with a fellow's will –
It's all in the state of mind.
If you think you're outclassed, you are
You've got to think high to rise
You've got to be sure of yourself before
You can ever win a prize.
Life's battles don't always go
To the stronger or faster man
But sooner or later the man who wins
Is the one who THINKS he can.

Where there is no vision
the people perish.

Ambition is not enough!
Climbing Everest without oxygen
is a step by step journey of devotion.

A new idea is first condemned as ridiculous
and then dismissed as trivial,
until finally, it becomes what everybody knows.

Listen for the voices of your visions;
they are nearby.

I prefer to be a dreamer among the humblest,
with visions to be realized,
than lord among those without dreams and desires.

WORK

Work – it has to be done! Most of us need to earn our daily bread. We need to produce and provide ourselves with the basic necessities such as food, clothes and shelter, and possibly a few luxuries besides. Our motivations for work may vary. Some people value work as an end in itself, such as the Protestant work ethic; others are committed to an organization, while others are committed to a career. Work takes place in a variety of differing social norms around the world. In Japan, for instance, work takes place in a hierarchical and paternalistic social structure; the Soviet countries worked in a centrally planned system. Whatever the culture work finds itself placed in, it still raises the same questions and performs the same functions for the society, and the individual also faces the same fundamental challenge – goal-directed behaviour.

Work gives us a sense of purpose and identity. Usually at a party or social gathering one of the first questions asked of someone is what they do; people become associated with their role in the manufacturing process. Some form of work is also necessary for mental health; we need to feel we have achieved something. Lack of work is ironically one of the most stressful experiences a person can have.

The problems associated with work are manifold. There is widespread discontent. Low job satisfaction, especially in repetitive unskilled work, lethargy, anxiety, stress, high blood pressure, overwork and boredom are all prevalent in the workplace. This occurs through a feeling of alienation derived from a lack of control over our workload. Work then becomes meaningless and unimportant. We lose our sense of community and shared social objectives. Apart from a radical reorganization of how industry and work are structured, how can we make our worklife more stimulating, challenging and rewarding?

Firstly, we may need to change our attitude to work. Some people still carry around the notion that earning our daily bread involves toiling on a treadmill pushing some grindstone – that work is devoid of pleasure and that any pleasure we do have should be crammed into any spare time we have. So we are led to believe. But we are worth much more than this. Others state that they do not enjoy pressure and stress; well, no matter what we do, we have to face these two beasts. If we set ourselves a target, somewhere along the line we will face them – they can't be ignored. The best way to deal with stress is to solve the problem – it won't go away. Actively tackling the problem reduces stress as you are actually doing something about it. There are also cynics who maintain that the objective of work is to earn as much as possible for as little work as possible. This idea can be held by employers who are only interested in exploitation, not only 'lethargic malcontents'. This view again ignores the fact that work can be rewarding and fulfilling. It doesn't have to be just a job that pays the rent. A great deal of our life is spent at work, so we need to concentrate on improving our situation as much as we can.

The aim of each of us, surely, is to work at the peak of efficiency and attain the goals we set ourselves. No one is satisfied by producing shoddy goods and services, nor in receiving them. Imagine what it would be like if you only produced quality work – and other companies did the same! The quality of our lives would improve dramatically and so many of life's petty frustrations would disappear. It's possible for all of us to make a real change and take an interest in what we do and as a result become more innovative, creative and valued workers to the benefit of everybody. Discover what you would really like to do. Time is needed to take a step back and review our situation and ourselves. The aim here is to gain clarity and insight. How can we improve our worklife? By having an aim and goal. Explore the possibilities open to you. What are your strengths and weaknesses? Do you enjoy working with people or computers? Suggest changes in working practices. Make the effort to learn a new skill. Change jobs. What is your temperament and character best suited for? Perseverance and a belief in yourself and a commitment to change will produce results. The old biblical saying, 'Knock and the door will be opened', will prove to be true.

When work ceases to be work but becomes a pleasure, we feel good and are more free to enjoy the other areas of our lives. We can return home without carrying the anxieties of our workplace with us. This has a direct influence on our relationships and social life, automatically relieving pressure.

*Do what you can
and the task will rest lightly
in your hand, so lightly
that you will be able
to look forward to the more difficult tests
which may be waiting for you.*

As you work,
so are you worked on.

The smallest deed is greater than
the grandest intention.

What is work?
And what is not work?

I look at my life as a good day's work.

Work is worship.

Work is love made visible.

The best soldier is not soldierly;
The best fighter is not ferocious;
The best conqueror does not take part in a war;
The best employer of men keeps himself below them.

Go quickly slowly.

A thousand years scarce serve to form a state;
An hour may lay it in the dust.

Make no little plans:
They have no magic to stir men's blood....
Make big plans,
aim high in hope and work.

What a man does;
that he has.

Results come from doing the right thing;
not from doing things right.

When the best student hears about the way
he practises it assiduously;
When the average student hears about the way
it seems to him one moment there,
and gone the next;
When the worst student hears about the way
he laughs out loud.
If he did not laugh
it would be unworthy of being the way.

This is the true joy in life,
the being used for a purpose
recognized by yourself as a mighty one,...
the being a force of Nature
instead of a feverish selfish little clod
of ailments and grievances
complaining that the world will not devote itself
to making you happy.

I am of the opinion that as long as I live
it is my privilege to do for the world whatever I can:
I want to be thoroughly used up when I die,
for the harder I work the more I live,
I rejoice in life for its own sake.
Life is no brief candle,
to me it's a sort of splendid torch,
which I've got to hold up for a moment
and I want to make it burn as brightly as possible
before handing it on to future generations.

HUMOUR

Humour is man's sixth sense. Humour is nature's most precious gift to man, as only human beings have a sense of humour. To be human, therefore, is to have a sense of humour.

Just as everyone is unique, we all have a unique smile, laugh and sense of humour. Humour is at the heart of being human. Humour is an umbrella term which includes smiling, chuckling, giggling, laughing. With humour we can create joy and happiness in our lives. It's simple: smile and the world will smile with you; laugh and happiness will surround you.

Laughter is the best medicine. Just like medicine, it has tangible effects on the mind, body and emotions. There is a proverb: 'Be happy – be healthy.' In other words, it is happiness which leads to health. We are taught that only after we have amassed wealth and health will we be happy. Not so! The fact is there are two kinds of people: the happy ones and those looking for reasons to be happy. Humour is the key which unlocks all the doors to happiness. It has the power to fuse tragedy and comedy.

Humour is the art of joyful living. To be childlike and experience the world without hurry, without worry. This is our natural state. As a child you did not get lessons on how to laugh – or cry, come to that. We laughed and cried naturally, spontaneously. In fact children often laugh until they cry and cry until they laugh. Crying and laughing make us shed tears! They are two sides of the same coin; and if we can't really laugh, we can't really cry. So if you can't really laugh, then cry. Or vice versa. Why? Because both crying and laughing are a form of self-cleansing (self-therapy). They leave us relaxed and feeling well. Crying and laughing are the most primal human activities. Remember? If you have forgotten, then it's time to relearn the ultimate secrets of life. You can start by asking yourself why you laugh or cry the way you do. Or, watch a child and it will show you how. Both crying and laughing occur on four levels. The first is superficial, the second is chesty, and the third deep from the belly ('belly up'). The fourth is hysterical and the whole body becomes 'paralysed', 'out of control', and even breathing has to wait. Then it starts again, and again. We even forget why we are crying or laughing and yet end up feeling completely relaxed.

The relaxing effects of crying and laughing occur

as a result of perpetual motion between tension, release, breath, tension and so on. Crying and laughing release surplus energy from the body and mind. The build-up from lack of expression, tension, frustration, anxiety and worry are vented. We get it 'out of our system' and feel physically and mentally relaxed. Our thoughts and emotions are like washed laundry: if not aired they stink! Laughter is the best way to clear the stink. A ten minute laugh or cry is equivalent to one hour's worth of therapy, or some deep relaxation technique. Laughter relaxes even the hardest most brutal person.

Beauty is a relaxed human being. Why? In a relaxed state we see and do things differently and with ease. Laughter has a profound effect on our perception of life. Humour alters our perspective and helps create a new one. Hence the old saying: 'People are disturbed not by things, but by the view they take of them.' We often have a laugh to escape the 'reality' of our situation, only to rest, relax and return to deal with it. People in extreme situations, like pioneers, adventurers or sick people often have a 'warped' sense of humour to raise themselves above the doldrums. A medieval poet once penned, 'Laughter takes us up, way high; from a bottomless pit, to the fresh, clear blue sky.'

When we are laughing we are truly alive. Yet a

full-bellied laugh is 'socially unacceptable'. It's not considered to be the done thing! How often have you seen your parents, teachers, politicians, priests and other people in positions of 'authority' showing themselves in a state of hysterical laughter – let alone crying? This attitude implies that full-bellied laughter is immature, even stupid. How sad, because laughter fires us with enthusiasm, inspiration and a sense of freedom from bondage. Laughter helps us to let go of what we're holding on to. It helps us endure and persevere in the darkest hour. When we laugh we lighten up and live.

So, learn to live by allowing yourself and others to laugh. You don't need an excuse to laugh. Just start with a cheeky smile, smirk and giggle, then chuckle and laugh. At first it will feel unreal. Keep going. After a while, one laugh will follow the next. Get into it! Laughter is contagious and soon everyone around you will be curled up with hysterical laughter.

He who laughs last
probably had it explained to him.

Do not take life too seriously.
You may never get out of it alive.

Learn to laugh
and you will learn to live.
Learn to cry
and you will learn to die.
Learn to love
and you will become immortal.

Life does not cease to be funny when people die
any more than it ceases to be funny
when people laugh.

There are two kinds of people in the world:
those who are happy;
and those who are looking for reasons to be happy.

Now that you have broken through the wall with your head, what will you do in the neighbouring cell?

A light heart lives longer.

There are some six billion of us —
all it would take to raise humanity out of darkness
is for everyone to come up with a joke.

At fifty, everyone has the face he deserves.

*Men will always be mad and those who
think they can cure them are the maddest of all.*

In a land of milk and honey
money would have jokes and smiling faces on it.

Humour is the first gift to perish
in a foreign tongue.

We participate in tragedy,
at comedy we only look.

Almost everything you will do will be insignificant,
but it is very important that you do it.

Experience is a good teacher,
but she sends in terrific bills.

A joy shared
is a joy doubled.

MYSELF

J ust be yourself!' We've all heard it said and it
sounds so simple yet, in reality, what does it mean
and how do we go about doing it? For being yourself
isn't just about how you present yourself to strangers.
It is also about the kind of life you have chosen to
live and the way in which you live it.

There was a time in our lives, for most of us it was
while we were still infants, when being ourselves was
not a concept or something to be striven for, it was
simply the way we were. It was a time when we were
content to 'simply be', living life in the moment. As
we grew older, our parents and those close to us
began pointing out things they didn't like about us,
the things they wanted to change and the dreams
and hopes they had for us. We began changing
ourselves to please them so that they would not
reject us.

For many, the process continues into adulthood,
until one day we realize that we don't know who we
are any more because we have spent so much time

trying to please others and 'fit in'. Our personality is a mismatch of the ideas, attitudes and beliefs held by family, friends and society at large and we may find that we have been trying to fulfil their hopes and dreams and not lived the life *we* wanted at all. For those who realize this, there is the chance to change and regain a sense of self and personal direction. The question then becomes: 'if I am not this jumble of other people's hopes, dreams and beliefs then who am I?' – a question which we all face at some point in our lives. Few, though, find a satisfactory answer that allows them to give up endlessly chasing fame and fortune and fulfil their inner needs so that they are content simply to 'be themselves'. At best, most of us end up trying to survive while looking forward to 'better days', which never seem to come.

> Life has its transitions.
> A seed must die to become a tree.
> A baby grows into a child,
> a child into an adult.
> Adults reach thirty years,
> then thirty-five and forty.
> What's beyond forty?
> Fifty, sixty and so it goes.

For those of us who search deeper and face

ourselves, at first all we find is loneliness, frustration, confusion, fatigue, fear, anxiety and depression all rolled into one – in short an 'Identity Crisis'. At times all you want to do is find a hole to curl up in and die. You think to yourself, 'Why me? What's wrong with me?' You realize that most of your life has been spent doing things not because you wanted to but because you had to. You never stopped for a moment to think: 'Why? ... Why am I doing these things? What am I doing with my life?' For the first time you are forced to take a deep look at the 'real you' that has been buried by the struggle to please and achieve. Slowly out of the confusion and continual self-questioning comes hope and a meaning for your life, unique to you. Life no longer feels unbearable and unmanageable. A rebirth takes place within you. For the first time you have an understanding of what it really means to 'be yourself'. As you let go of the attitudes, ideas and expectations of others, you begin to be in touch with your own needs and are able to separate them from the needs of those around you.

The questions then become: 'What do I like and dislike about myself? What do I change and leave about myself? What direction do I take my life in? What am I motivated by?' In answering these questions you slowly are able to accept all parts of yourself and nurture rather than force your own development. The chase is ended and replaced by an inner stillness which allows you to be content with 'being' rather than 'becoming'. As the stillness you have found deepens, so does your understanding of being yourself and being human. The journey of life no longer seems a dark and lonely road, but a joyful path full of mystery and wonder. Each step is a step towards knowing yourself. To have this feeling is to know your true power and purpose in being human. For to 'know thyself' is the ultimate wisdom.

To love oneself
is the beginning of a life-long romance.

The price of dishonesty is self-destruction.

CHARACTERISTICS OF LIVING

1. *We have a body.*
2. *We can learn lessons.*
3. *There are no mistakes, only lessons.*
4. *A lesson repeats itself until it is learned.*
5. *Learning lessons does not end.*
6. *'There' is no better than 'here'.*
7. *Others are mirrors of us.*
8. *What I do is my responsibility.*
9. *There is only one constant – change.*
10. *The answer is inside us.*
11. *We shall forget all this.*
12. *We can remember it when we want.*

Just trust yourself.
Then you will know how to live.

We have met the enemy – and he is us.

All men dream;
but not equally.
Those who dream by night
in the dusty recesses of their minds
wake in the day to find it vanity;
but the dreamers of the day are dangerous men,
for they act their dreams with open eyes,
to make it possible.

The cruellest lies are often told in silence.

In each one of us there is a king,
speak to him and he will come forth.

It is a secret place,
the land of tears.

Give me a firm place to stand
and I will move the earth.

To be a public man is slavery.

Self-hurt is planetary hurt,
Self-nurturance is planetary nurturance.

Every seed must die
before it can become a plant.

The fault, dear Brutus, is not in our stars;
but in ourselves;
that we are underlings.

I am not what you call me
I am what I answer to.

No one can please everyone.
Your mental peace is more important.
If you are in peace
then others around you will feel peace.
So your best efforts
should be to work on yourself.

SOURCES OF THE INSPIRATIONS

148

FURTHER READING

Bach, Richard, *Jonathan Livingstone Seagull*, Turnstone Press Ltd., 1972.

Bek, Lilla, with Pullar, Philippa, *To The Light*, Unwin Paperbacks, 1985.

Castenada, Carlos, *The Power of Silence*, Pocket Books, 1988.

Chang, Dr Stephen T., *Chinese Self-Healing*, Aquarian Press, 1986.

Dethlefsen, T. and Dahlke, R., *The Healing Power of Illness*, Element Books Ltd., 1990.

Ferrucci, Piero, *What We May Be*, Turnstone Press, 1988.

Gawain, Shakti, *Reflections in the Light*, New World Library, 1988.

Gibran, Kahlil, *The Prophet*, William Heinemann Ltd., 1926.

Hay, Louise, *You Can Heal Your Life*, Eden Grove Publications, 1988.

Janov, Dr Arthur, *The Feeling Child*, Abacus, 1982.

Kapleau, Philip, *The Three Pillars of Zen*, Beacon Press, 1967.

Kübler-Ross, Elisabeth, *Death the Final Stage of Growth*, Simon and Schuster, 1986.

Orr, Leonard and Ray, Sondra, *Rebirthing in the New Age*, Celestial Arts, 1977.

Roman, Sanaya, and Packer, Duane, *Creating Money – Keys to Abundance*, H. J. Kramer Inc., 1988.

Schiff, Francine, *Food For Solitude*, Element Books, 1992.

Scott Peck, M., *The Road Less Travelled*, Rider (London), Simon and Schuster (USA), 1978.

Stoler Miller, Barbara (trans.), *The Bhagavad–Gita*, Bantam Books, 1986.

White Eagle, *The Quiet Mind*, The White Eagle Publishing Trust, 1972.